Cats in Flats

Written and illustrated by
KAREN CHAMBERS

Trafford PUBLISHING® www.trafford.com

North America & international
toll-free: 1 888 232 4444 (USA & Canada)
phone: 250 383 6864 ♦ fax: 812 355 4082

For Alex and Nick

and all the wonderful

feline friends

who have graced our lives

with their mischievous

and knowing

ways.

Hush,

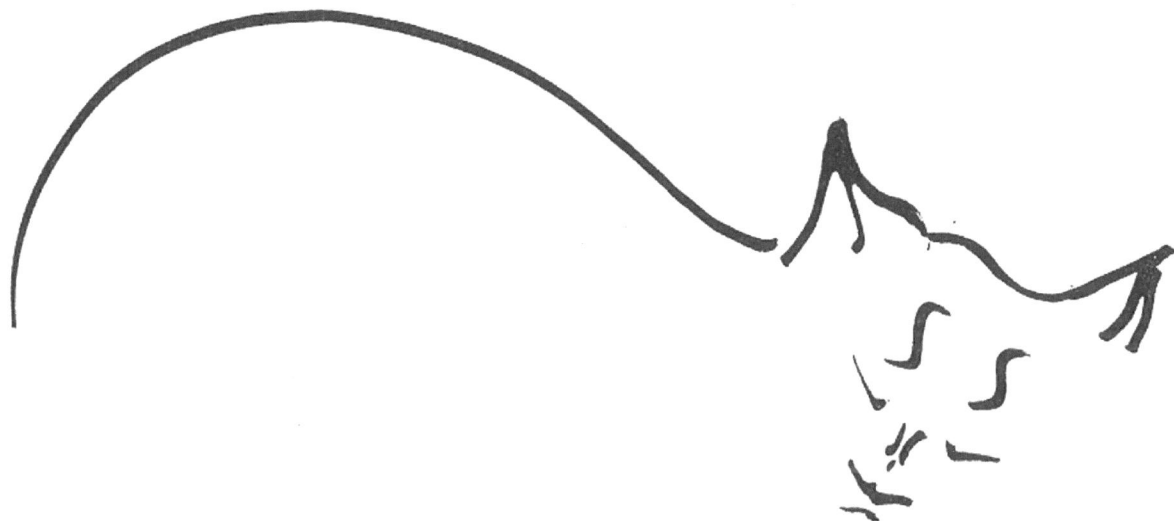

Quiet...

...there's a cat
in the flat.
A CAT!
In the flat.
Oh no!
Never that.

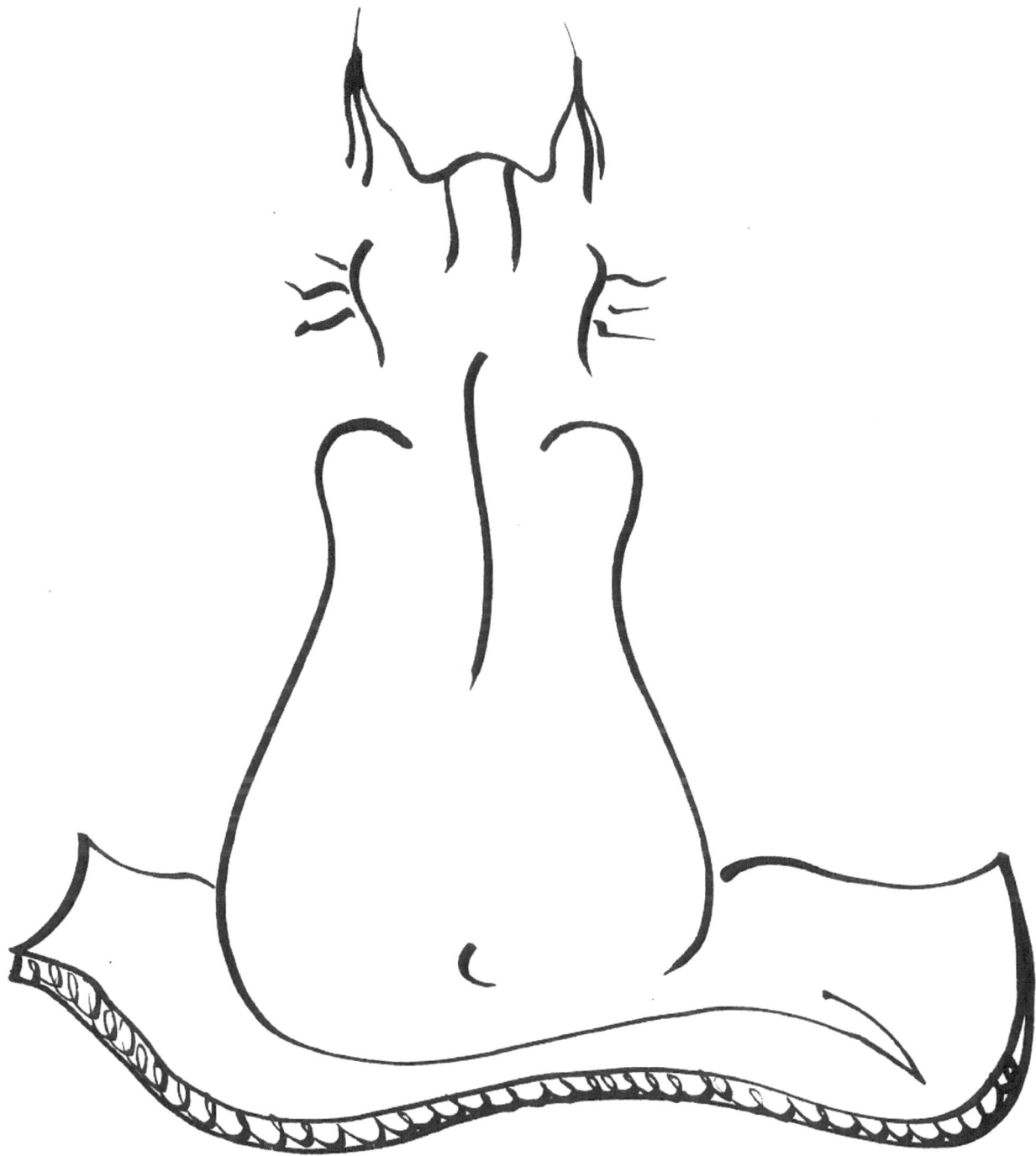

Oh dear!   Oh dear!
  They're not allowed
  Here-

(That's what the man said)

  Come quickly,
  Oh hurry,
    Get him out of my bed!

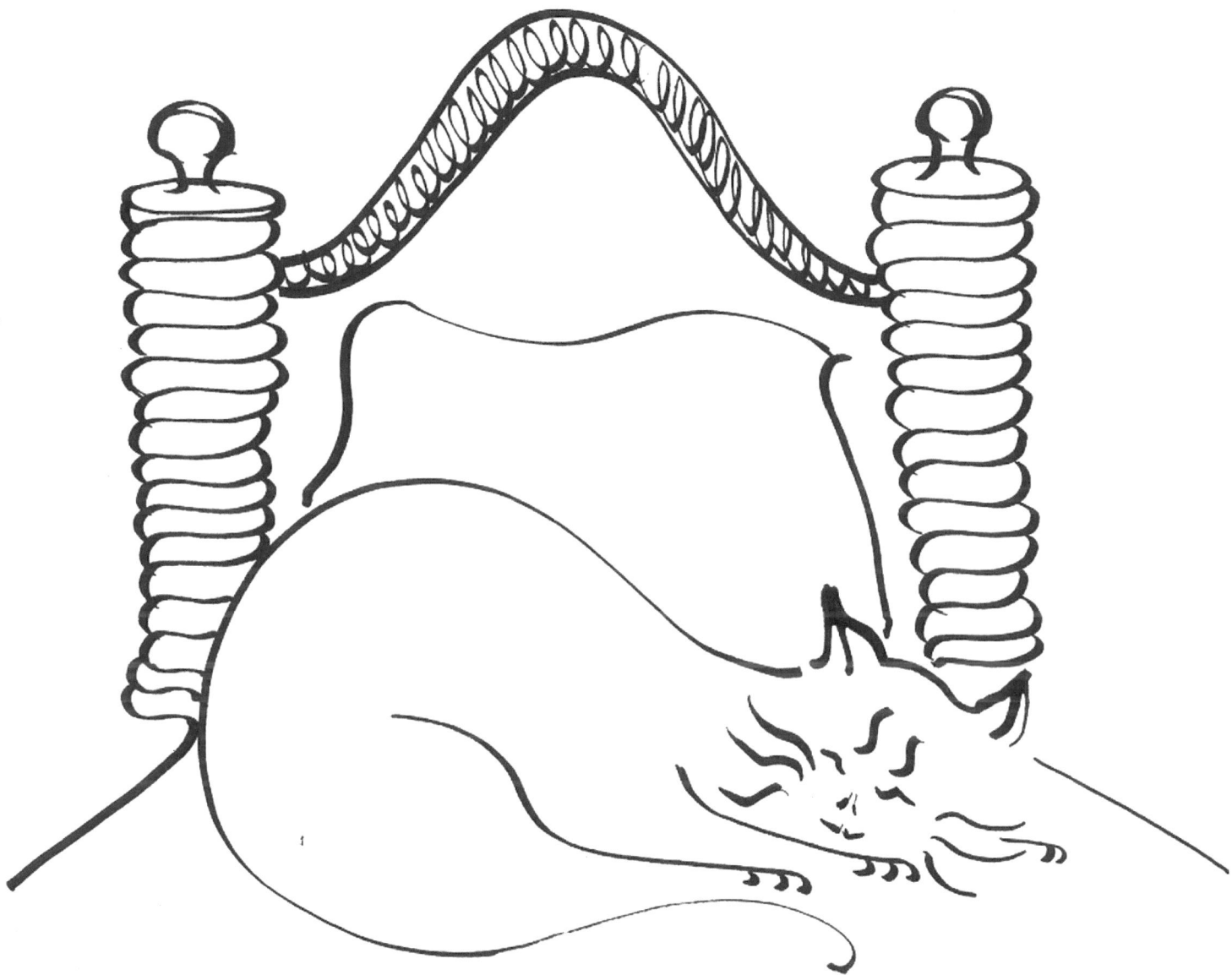

But wait:-
    There are places
        We could find for him.
            If he rolled very small
                He could hide-
                    In the bin.

Or maybe
  A lampshade
    He could be:
      No-one would notice,
        No-one would see.

But wait,
Where is he?
Did we give him
A fright?
He's not in the bin,
Nor
under the light.

Look carefully,
    Yes carefully
       look at our mat !
          For in its soft colours,
(The colours of dawn)
          Hides our ginger cat
        Snug, cosy
          and warm.

So of course

   We can keep him

      For who'd ever know,

         That in this mat

            Which we proudly show ,

               Hides

                  The cat

                     In our flat!

My "Finding Cats Poem"

When I tread very softly,
   The cats that I see are
   Up the …
   On the …
   In the …
Between the…

   Behind the...
   Down the …
   Under the …

My "Finding Cats Poem"

But most of all,

With …

Maggie "world watching" from the windowsill

My Favourite Cat Drawing

www.ingramcontent.com/pod-product-compliance
Lightning Source LLC
LaVergne TN
LVHW072123070426

835511LV00002B/78